OUT WITH THE OLD

TRACEY BOND

Requests for information should be addressed to: Tracey Bond, Pullpenz.com
DeKalb, IL 60115

Copyright (C) 2017 by Tracey Bond

All rights reserved. This book publication is protected by the copyright laws of the United States of America. This book may not be copied or reprinted for commercial gain or profit. With proper annotation credit given, the use of short quotations for personal or group study is permitted and warmly encouraged. Permission will be granted upon formal request.

Please note that Pullpenz.com 's compilation style capitalizes certain words, pronouns, et. als, to convey the emotional emphasis of the author's thoughtful expression point(s), that may differ from other publishers' styles.

This publication is designed to share expert information about the subject matter covered in the public relations and communications industry for coaching guidance, and consultation values as a thoughtful commentary. It is sold with the understanding that the author and/or publisher is not engaged in rendering legal, accounting, financial, mental health and/or wellness, psychological, or other professional advice beyond spiritual counsel based on relevant experience expertise. If legal advice or other expert assistance is required, beyond the scope of the author's expertise; the service of a qualified professional person should be sought.

Book Concept, Cover & Interior Design, Author Headshot & Layout by Tracey Bond, Executive Book Producer at Pullpenz.com

For Worldwide Distribution, Printed in the U.S.A.
Reach us on the Internet at: Pullpenz.com
For information about special discounts available for bulk purchases, sales promotions, fund-raising and educational needs, contact Pullpenz.com Sales at 1-707-271-6171 x. 2 or Pullpenz..com.

OUT WITH THE OLD
TREND INTO YOUR NEW!

TRACEY BOND

OUT WITH THE OLD
TREND INTO YOUR NEW!

Oh why can't the neuro-bliss of a coming new year, last longer than Christmas cheer? I don't know how you value numbers – and I'm no numerologist. I do know that numbers carry values for many reasons as well as seasons. The more I've paid them attention to them, the more fascinating they've become. I've seen their significance when recorded historical documents like the bible scriptures, to identify, measure and even plan special times.

Two numbers I'm particularly giddy about are seven (&), and eight (8). Why? The number 7 precedes 8 as a *finishing* number. In fact these 2 numbers happen to make up my birthdate in 3 numerical places. Not only does fits well with the full completeness of something like a great finish; but a great finish should precede a timing for newness, 8 symbolizes. 8 has a relationship to resurrection of old/dead things previous, new birth, new life, and great *beginnings*! 8 couldn't show up any better on a calendar than for New Years Day.

At the time of this publication, 8 will serve as the finishing number for the new year. I can't resist sharing a few of my not-so-secret agent insights as a publicist to help you transform out of your last year mindset into your new action plans.
By recycling and renewing the energy build up during high-spirited holiday times, symbols like these can create meaningful significance for future planning. I hope you take some legitimate time to identify symbols you can integrate into some attractive dialogue about your new revelations - those can help reinforce great resolutions. Right before every New Year, it is amazing how quickly our minds process out of the "Christmas spirit" during the holiday season. With the blink-per-click speed of a social media post, it seems every business-minded entrepreneur should be ready to switch gears too, right?

Just like everyone else using their personal technology devices to scroll along with the end-of-year media-cultured buzz about what's next on people's New Year 'to do list' for profitability and productivity. I'm willing to bet that making more money in the New Year, is a list-topper!

Speaking of more money, what do you think about that rhetorical term new money? "Ain't nothin' like new money!" Are you thinking about what you're gonna do to make some new year money? What does the term mean to YOU? Does it mean you're lookin' like you're coming into something new...not outdated like a past year, but like you're coming into something new, sought after like good fortune, to increase YOU?

Tracey Bond

OUT WITH THE OLD

✦✦ TREND INTO YOUR NEW!

TRACEY BOND

OUT WITH THE OLD
TREND INTO YOUR NEW!

When you appear to people like the meaning of the common phrase 'new money,' you appear crisp and sharp...its as prosperous a compliment as it is, commentary! I mean everything is clean, fresh and clean on you. In other words, you look like you have come into a fortunate season - all brand new! That perception of you... emergence out an old situation, into some beautiful newness has the effect of creating value and interest in the minds of your audience about you.

Now is a great time to take a serious look at your business buzz, and consider the value of re-purposing your old communication style with your brand and audiences. Speak out and publish your NEW...and let the whole world review!

"Out with the old, TREND into YOUR New!"

It doesn't matter if you're an author, coach, artist, a CEO, small or large business owner, you may be an expert business consultant, and otherwise a professional at what you do. If you are in business for yourself - say it after me "It is time to *grow* out with the old and TREND-ing with MY NEW. Say it, say it: "MY NEW!" Let your whole bodyscape {*a word I made up just now* :)} hear you say real loud, "MY NEW!" Doesn't that excite you, just to speak it...then really hear it with your mindset? If it does not excite you to hear yourself speak it over your future. If your spirit has reached a settlement agreement with your mindset, concluding that it is enough for you to have physically survived the previous year, you're unlikely to communicate any new views easily. If you're in business and you have no excitement at this time of year about something new about you and what you're producing, NOW is the time to really take a sober look at what is growing good with you, and closer at the communication root of your business growth.

A unique first look I like to take with my virtual public relations clientele is through audience exposure dynamic of trending. YESSSS, and I do mean TRENDING hot like everybody's resolution buzz on the first day of a NEW YEAR.

With an attitude of 'everyday-is-a-holiday' cheer, I want to influence you to be resolute in a commitment to consistently, and publicly communicate your exodus out the old, so you may TREND into your NEW!

Tracey Bond

OUT WITH THE OLD

TREND INTO YOUR NEW!

TRACEY BOND

OUT WITH THE OLD
TREND INTO YOUR NEW!

The word *'trend'* found its origins as a noun, being something that bends, and definitely not how we *'trend'* to think it should mean today. We use the word trend quite often to categorize something that is popular currently pertaining to news, and/or of identifiable public interest at a particular time and season.

By the late 1800's trend was used as a course or direction of something, like the round or bend in the layout of a river or perhaps a road.

In this age of social media, the prevalent tendency to use a word like 'trend' in our culture, our news, fashion or whatever is to make it remarkable. When we say something is trending – we mean to say that something is evolving in a consistent noticeable way. Other words have emerged from the usage of trend, words like trendy, and trendsetter evolve from that.

Where do you fit in with that term trending? If you're in business with people for productivity, then your market audience, consumer and clients should be able to easily locate where you're 'trending' for themselves in their online or offline quests for your *newness*?

Newness is almost at the core of many retail markets that depend heavily on newness to survive. If you have some scriptural wisdom, and I am not slighting anyone that doesn't understand – just trying to make a mental connection here for understanding with the wisdom scriptures in the 1st chapter of Ecclesiastes, where Solomon (reputation of being the wisest man that walked the earth) said with simplicity "...there's nothing NEW under the sun."

What does that mean there's nothing new under the sun? It means that almost everything that has been materially created has been set in place...that even includes you. Sure, there may be new discoveries, scientific research – developments with technology that explains how something old can be improved upon to work better; but inventions and developments are produced from things (materials) already existed from the foundations of the old earth.

In an opening Ecclesiastes scriptural quotation reference in Chapter 1: verse 9, Solomon reasoned about life from a perspective, saying: "What has been will be again, what has been done will be done again; there is nothing new under the sun." So in that context, we get how history is set for repetition.

TRACEY BOND

OUT WITH THE OLD

TREND INTO YOUR NEW!

TRACEY BOND

OUT WITH THE OLD
TREND INTO YOUR NEW!

When it comes to retail markets though, if you don't repackage, and develop new communications (scripts, marketing messages, media conversations, press releases, etc., around celebrating your product; audiences are apt to get bored and lose interest quickly.

I'm not talking about a product like toilet-paper. I don't know how much more we can revolutionize toilet paper unless we develop some kind of artificial intelligence (AI) that unwraps it for us, unrolls it, and measures the length, ply-count for absorption, numerical sheet count, etc. for routine excretory management...(not the best analogy, but I hope you see the point). There's nothing new in that context of creations.

Some things are made without sophistication for common and disposable purposes for throwing out...but somethings are made for higher purposes like activities, concepts, ideas, events, plans and products for bringing in.

We need *newness* as a signal to ourselves and our respective audiences that not only has a change out of the old come forth; but it comes trending newness to keep us going, growing and glowing. Struggling with motives for embracing newness. Think for a moment about how the earth renews itself!

As *old* as we've learned to believe our Earth is, we know it sustains our habitation with cycles of environmental changes.

"The sun still shines on Summer's leaves as Spring's leaves grow old, and Fall's weather grows cold. Fall seasons sweep them up and them out, while Winter communicates with cool winds. Snowflakes break their news release to the Earth, announcing its time to trend the season's way in; while 'mediarologists' report the fact updates & histories about weather's who, what why, how and when."
~ Tracey Bond #Weatherquotes #PrQuotes

During Winter seasons, a tree's planted root systems grow deep into warmer Earth, supplying, signaling and sending up, out and forth the resources needed to pronounce Spring's newness in again.

That is nature's reminder to us that even seasons use coordinated and systematic communication to trend their new productions in the land.

Tracey Bond

OUT WITH THE OLD

✦ TREND INTO
YOUR NEW!

TRACEY BOND

OUT WITH THE OLD
TREND INTO YOUR NEW!

Think! What new things can your audiences count on you for through in your business cycles in the new year?

What's new with you should always have a consistent and cyclical way of shining through your managed communications too.

Focus on framing your newness on platforms you haven't leveraged; knowing our audiences want to engage us there – the way they want to.

The moment you start resets your 'newness' communication clock!

Are you ready to learn how transcend out of the old, to transform how you communicate your newness ideas, goals and plans for success in the new year?

Need help? I'm here to cheer you new-ward!
* Email me today at: traceybond@traceybond007.com

HASHTAG: OUTWITHTHEOLD

SIGN UP AT PULLPENZ.COM PUBLISHING FOR BOOK EVENT UPDATES, MASTERCLASS TRAINING, VIP DAYS, MEDIA INTERVIEWS & SPEAKER LEADERSHIP OPPORTUNITIES

PULLPENZ.COM | @PULLPENZ | #PULLPENZ

OUT WITH THE OLD

TREND INTO YOUR NEW!

TRACEY BOND

OUT WITH THE OLD

TREND INTO YOUR NEW!

TRACEY BOND'S AMAZON AUTHOR PAGE

 https://www.amazon.com/Tracey-Bond/e/B00KVM1LVO

FOLLOW TRACEY BOND ON HER AMAZON AUTHOR PAGE FOR ALL HER PUBLISHED BOOKS

HASHTAG: TRACEYBOND007
@TRACEY007BOND

OUT WITH THE OLD

✦ TREND INTO
YOUR NEW!

TRACEY BOND

OUT WITH THE OLD

 # TREND INTO YOUR NEW!

"everybody has a story lets pull yours out together!" - Pullpenz.com

PEOPLESTORIESMATTER

https://www.pullpenz.com

 EMAIL: PULLPENZ GMAIL.COM

HASHTAG: PULLPENZ
@PULLPENZ

OUT WITH THE OLD

TREND INTO YOUR NEW!

Tracey Bond

OUT WITH THE OLD

TREND INTO YOUR NEW!

"Coaching is the intuitive adventure of influence...the help you gift to yourself."
~ Tracey Bond

BOOK TRACEY BOND FOR ONLINE SOCIAL BUSINESS COACHING

BOOK YOUR SIGNATURE SOCIAL BUSINESS COACHING CONSULTATION WITH COACH BOND NOW!

https://beneficience.pr.checkappointments.com

 HASHTAG: TRACEYBOND007

TRACEYBOND007.COM

OUT WITH THE OLD
✦ TREND INTO
YOUR NEW!

TRACEY BOND

OUT WITH THE OLD

TREND INTO YOUR NEW!

Complimentary Consultations

BENEFICIENCE.COM
VIRTUAL & PROLIFIC
PERSONAGE PR

https://www.beneficience.com

BENEFICIENCE.COM VIRTUAL PR MAKES YOUR PR NEWS HEADLINES NONSTOP!

HASHTAG: BENEFICIENCE PR

@BENEFICIENCE #VirtualPr

OUT WITH THE OLD
✦ TREND INTO
YOUR NEW!

TRACEY BOND

OUT WITH THE OLD

 # TREND INTO YOUR NEW!

JOIN TRACEY BOND TUESDAYS FOR SPEAKINTOTHEPODLIGHT'S LETS # TALKONTUESDAY SHOW

https://www.blogtalkradio.com/speakintothepodlight

FOLLOW TRACEY BOND ON HER MEDIAPHILIC PRRADIO SHOW & PODCAST.
TO LEARN HOW YOU CAN BECOME A GUEST – VISIT WWW.PEAKINTOTHEPODLIGHT.COM

 HASHTAG: SPEAKINTOTHEPODLIGHT

TRACEY BOND

OUT WITH THE OLD

TREND INTO YOUR NEW!

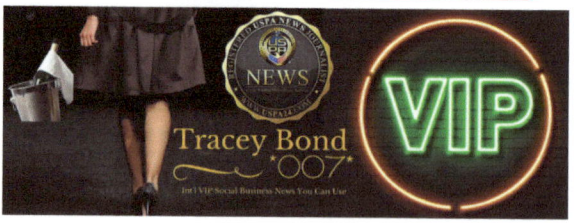

LEARN MORE ABOUT BESTSELLING ENTREPRENEURSHIP AUTHOR & AWARDED HOLLYWOOD VIRTUAL PUBLICIST TRACEY BOND

https://epodcastnetwork.com/public-relations-conversations-with-tracey-bond-girl-a-real-life-pr-double-agent-on-intl-womens-day/

CLICK THE URL LINK ABOVE TO HEAR TRACEY BOND'S MEDIAPRENEURSHIP INTERVIEW ON EPODCASTNETWORK

 LINKED IN: #TRACEYBOND007

INSTAGRAM #TRACEYBOND007

OUT WITH THE OLD

TREND INTO YOUR NEW!

TRACEY BOND

www.ingramcontent.com/pod-product-compliance
Lightning Source LLC
Chambersburg PA
CBHW040312220526
45473CB00002B/640